LITTLE LAMBS BIBLE STORYTIME

WITH QUIZZES, VOLUME 1

Donna A. Hackett

Table of Contents

THE LIE THAT WENT WRONG

Little one, many people believe it is okay to lie. Many even get away with lying. Some do not stop to think about God before they tell a lie. Let's go to the Bible and look at a story that will show you what God thinks about lying, even if people believe they are lying for a good cause. In 1 Kings 14, we are told of king Jeroboam of Israel. His son Abijah was sick. Jeroboam told his wife (the queen), "Come, change your clothes so that no one will know it's you, and go to Shiloh. There you will find the prophet Ahijah; ask him what is to happen to our child." So Jeroboam's wife changed her clothes and went to the house of Ahijah, who could no longer see, as he was an old man. But before she got there, the Lord told his prophet what Jeroboam and his wife were planning—how she was to come to see him, pretending to be someone else. The Lord also told Ahijah what to say to her.

Not long after this, Ahijah the prophet heard the sound of Jeroboam's wife as she came in through the door. Before she even said one word to him, Ahijah gave her the message from God. She was to go and tell her husband, king Jeroboam, that even though God made him king over the ten tribes of Israel, Jeroboam had not kept God's commandments like God's servant David had. Instead, Jeroboam did more evil than any other king before him. He made false gods for the people to worship, instead of worshipping the true God of heaven. Because Jeroboam turned his back on God, God was to bring evil on his house and destroy all who were related to him. So terrible was Jeroboam's betrayal that God said he was going to let dogs, and fowls of the air, eat the dead bodies of Jeroboam's relatives.

Ahijah the prophet continued by saying that this was not all. As soon as Jeroboam's wife returned to her own house, her son Abijah would die. Abijah would be the only relative of king Jeroboam who would be buried in a grave, as the Lord saw some good in him.

Little one, can you imagine that? Here you are, having come to lie to a blind man, and yet he tells you more than you had ever dreamed would happen. You see, many people think very little of God's servants. Some think that it is easy to fool those who serve God. These people may lie, steal, or spread rumors, but they do not stop to think that our heavenly Father sees everything. He will protect and watch over his faithful servants as the apples of his eye. We see that the king and the queen tried to deceive and use trickery, but to their own destruction. Even though this story is in the Bible to teach us, as words of warning, many people overlook them to live as they please. They forget that God is in control and that one day they too will meet with the wrath of God.

Little one, learn this lesson now! God is not pleased with lying, for no liar can enter heaven. Satan, the Devil, is the greatest liar, and he can never go back to heaven. So come to Jesus now, and ask him to help you to tell the truth always. Even though the life of a true Christian is not a popular one, little one, you must be true to God, come what may. Amen.

Quiz #1

1) Where in the Bible does this story appear? _____

2) Who was the king of Israel at this time? _____

3) What did the king tell his wife to change? _____

4) What could the prophet Ahijah not do anymore because of his age? _____

5) Who told Ahijah that the queen was coming to see him? _____

6) Can we hide what we do, say, or think from God? _____

7) Who was the only one of Jeroboam's relatives to be buried? _____

8) Which king did God say kept his commandments? _____

9) What did king Jeroboam cause the people to do? _____

10) When did Abijah die? _____

11) Who is the greatest liar? _____

12) If we tell lies, where will we not be able to go? _____

13) Should we be friends with those who are liars? _____

Little one, the people we choose as our friends can teach us to do good or evil, so we must be careful in whom we choose as friends. Being a friend to a liar might teach you to lie. Do you know whom to pick as your friend? If you don't, pray and ask Jesus to tell you. He will always guide you toward what is right.

Inspirational Quote

"Parents must exercise unceasing watchfulness, that their children be not lost to God. The vows of David, recorded in the 101ˢᵗ Psalm, should be the vows of all upon whom rest the responsibilities of guarding the influences of the home. The psalmist declares: "I will set no wicked thing before mine eyes: I hate the work of them that turn aside; it shall not cleave to me. A froward heart shall depart from me: I will not know a wicked person. Whoso privily slandereth his neighbour, him will I cut off: him that hath an high look and a proud heart will not I suffer. Mine eyes shall be upon the faithful of the land, that they may dwell with me: he that walketh in a perfect way, he shall serve me. He that worketh deceit shall not dwell within my house: he that telleth lies shall not tarry in my sight" (Ellen G. White, *The Adventist Home* [Hagerstown: Review and Herald Publishing Association, 1952], page 408)

A Bad Choice

Little ones, have you seen others who have a lot of material things yet are not happy? These are the people who always want more—and they do not share what they have with others. Jesus told the story of a rich young ruler in Mark 10:17–22. The ruler had much wealth. One day, he watched Jesus bless some children whom the disciples had tried to drive away. After Jesus finished and was on his way, the young man ran to Jesus and fell on his knees, asking, "Good Master, what shall I do to inherit eternal life?" This ruler had a high position in the temple, but he felt that there was something missing in his life. So after watching Jesus bless the children, he desired to be blessed by Jesus as well.

Jesus answered by pointing out how one can receive eternal life, by keeping the commandments. To this, the ruler said, "All this I have done from my youth; what lack I yet?"

Jesus told the man his true condition. "There is one thing that you are missing." He was missing the love of God in his heart. So Jesus placed before him a choice, essentially asking him, "How badly do you want eternal life?" Jesus said to the man, "Go thy way, sell whatsoever thou hast, and give to the poor, and thou shalt have treasure in heaven: and come, take up the cross, and follow Me" (Mark 10:21). The choice that the ruler had to make was between having a great deal of worldly goods and having heavenly treasure. In order to have heavenly treasure or eternal life, he had to take up the cross and follow Jesus on the path where he would have to place his wants after his obedience to God.

Upon hearing what it took to receive eternal life, the rich young ruler became sad. He sorrowfully went away from Jesus. He had great possessions. This young man was rich in this world's goods, and he could not bring himself to part with his riches in order to be a disciple of Christ. Instead, he chose to keep his riches and let go of Jesus.

What about you, little one? Do you hang on to things in your life that will cause you to be parted from Jesus? The rich young ruler said, "I have kept all of the Father's commandments from my youth," but this was not true. The first commandment reads, "Thou shalt have no other gods before Me." The wealth of this young man had become an idol to him, as he chose riches over serving God. May God help us to always keep him first in our life. Amen!

Quiz #2

1) Where in the Bible does this story appear? _____

2) Who wanted to be blessed by Jesus? _____

3) What question did he ask of Jesus? _____

4) For this person to receive eternal life, what would he have to keep? _____

5) How many choices did Jesus put before the ruler? _____

6) In order to follow Jesus, what would the young man have to do? _____

7) What choice did he make? _____

8) How did his choice make him feel? _____

9) Did his feelings help him make the right choice? _____

10) What was the young ruler missing in his life? _____

Little one, will you also go away from Jesus so you can have this world's goods? Yes or no?

Inspirational Quote

"The lover of self is a transgressor of the law. This Jesus desired to reveal to the young man, and He gave him a test that would make manifest the selfishness of his heart. He showed him the plague spot in his character. The young man desired no further enlightenment. He had cherished an idol in the soul; the world was his god" (Ellen G. White, *Christ's Object Lessons* [Washington: Review and Herald Publishing Association, 1900], page 392)

A Special Book

Little one, we have a most special book called the Holy Bible. Many people own a copy of this book. They value its teachings and try to live their lives by obeying it. However, others say that the Bible is just a common book, that there's nothing special about it. Still others say that ordinary men and women wrote the Bible, so there is no need to obey it. But the truth is that the Bible was written by more than forty people over a span of sixteen hundred years. Some of the writers were fishermen, tax collectors, tentmakers, shepherds, prophets, or generals, while others were kings. They were from different places in the world and wrote in Hebrew, Aramaic, or Greek. They wrote about many different things; yet all the subjects that they wrote about were in agreement with each other. It was as if the words that they wrote all came from the same person.

Do you know how we came to have all of the writings of the Bible collected in one book, little one? It was through the invention of a machine called the printing press around the year 1450. The inventor was a German man named Johannes Gutenberg. This machine was used to print and make books. For the first time ever, it was possible to print books in large numbers. Before this, everything had to be handwritten, and it took a very long time to produce copies. Since this printing press was the first machine of its kind in the whole world, which book do you think people chose to be the first printed book? If you guessed the Bible, then you guessed right! The Bible was the first book ever printed. Since then, more people have read the Bible. It has been printed more times than any other book in history.

Through the help of Bible societies, over one billion Bibles had been scattered around the world by 1930. But God was not yet finished with getting his word out around the world, because by 1977 these Bible societies printed more than two hundred million Bibles every year. In addition to the societies that printed these copies, there were other publishing companies that also printed the Bible. This means, little one, that anyone in the world who was interested in knowing more about God's word, how to live, what God expects of us, etc., could get a Bible and read what it says for themselves in their own language. "What do you mean, in their own language?" you ask. The Bible is not only in English or a few languages; rather, it has been translated into more than fourteen hundred languages. No other book has even come close to being so important as the Bible.

Has anyone ever tried to destroy the Bible? Oh yes. Sometime near the year 300 AD, the Roman emperor Diocletian gave an order for all Bibles to be burned. He thought that by doing this he could get rid of

Christianity. Anyone who was caught with a Bible was to be killed. Also, there was a French philosopher named Voltaire (1694–1778) who did not believe in God. Voltaire's writings destroyed the faith of many people because his words caused them to doubt that what the Bible said was true. This man was so sure of himself that he boasted that a hundred years after he died, the Bible would disappear from the earth. History tells us that Voltaire died in 1778, whereas the Bible did not disappear but continued to live. Do you want to know how foolish this man's boast was? About fifty years after Voltaire died, the Geneva Bible Society moved into his old house and used his printing presses to print thousands of Bibles. Little one, truly we see that God is in control of his words and that no person can destroy them. We also see how foolish it is to fight against God. Amen!

Quiz #3

1) About how many people wrote the Bible? _____

2) What was invented in the year 1450? _____

3) The Bible was written over a period of how many years? _____

4) What was the first printed book in the world? _____

5) Has there been any other book more widely printed in the world than the Bible? _____

6) What did the Roman emperor Diocletian order in 300 AD? _____

7) What did Emperor Diocletian hope to destroy? _____

8) Who said that within a hundred years after his death, the Bible would disappear? _____

9) Who moved into that person's house fifty years after his death? _____

10) Has there be any person alive or dead who has succeeded in destroying the Bible? _____

11) Who invented the first printing press? _____

Are you thankful to have a Bible? You are? Then let us read more of it!

Inspirational Quote

"Children should be taught to reject trashy, exciting tales and to turn to sensible reading, which will lead the mind to take an interest in Bible story, history, and argument" (Ellen G. White, *The Adventist Home* [Hagerstown: Review and Herald Publishing Association, 1952], page 417)

FULL OF PRIDE

Hello, little one. Do you have friends who are forceful, who always want to have their own way? Do these friends refuse to listen? Some of these people even believe that because they have money, they can do whatever they please. Do you think that is right? Well, let's see from this story.

There was a king in Israel whose name was Uzziah. At sixteen years old, he was made king. Wow! At that age, did he know how to rule a country? The Bible tells us that he did what was right in the sight of the Lord, based on what he had learned from his father, Amaziah. Hmm! Child, do you see how important it is to have parents who love the Lord, parents who will teach their children to love God as well? How about you, little one; do you love God? Are you willing to do what is right in his sight?

Uzziah obeyed God. As long as he did this, God gave him success in whatever he did. How did God help him? He helped the king when he went to war against his enemies, the Philistines and the Arabians. What did king Uzziah do for his country? He built towers in Jerusalem and strengthened them; he built towers in the desert; and he dug many wells, as he had a lot of cattle. Plus, he had many soldiers who were very organized. He also gave his soldiers many weapons. But he did not stop there. Uzziah made engines in Jerusalem that had been invented by skillful men. He then placed these engines on the towers to shoot arrows and great stones at any enemies. Because of this, his fame spread far and wide, as never before had such a thing as this been done. How did Uzziah know how to do this? Some might say that he was a smart man, brilliant. Little one, don't you believe that. Jesus says to us in John 15:5, "I am the vine, ye are the branches: He that abideth in me, and I in him, the same bringeth forth much fruit: *for without me ye can do nothing*" (emphasis added). The Bible says in 2 Chronicles 26:15 that king Uzziah was marvelously helped until he was made strong. Yes, little one, God helped Uzziah with these ideas and also helped make them come true. This made Uzziah a strong king, with a strongly defended country.

With all this success, Uzziah must have been very close to God. True, but let's see what happens next. The Bible says that when Uzziah was strong, his heart was lifted up, to his destruction. Pride took a hold of him. He got to the point where he thought he could do no wrong—and no one could tell him otherwise. And so he went into the temple of God to burn incense, which was a work that only the priests were assigned to do.

The priest Azariah went inside after the king with eighty other priests who were strong men. They stood up to the king, telling him not to burn incense to God, as that was not the work of a king, but of a priest. "Go out of here," they said, "for you have sinned against God. This does not honor God." How did Uzziah react to this? He became very angry. While he had a censer for burning incense in his hand, leprosy rose up on his forehead before the priests, the Bible tells us. When the priests saw this, they knew that God had smitten Uzziah, so they pushed him out of the temple. Little one, from that point forward, king Uzziah remained a leper until he died. May God help us to be obedient to Him and put away pride before we end up rebelling like king Uzziah.

QUIZ #4

1) Where in the Bible is this story found? _____

2) How old was Uzziah when he became king? _____

3) Why did God give Uzziah success in what he did? _____

4) Name two things that Uzziah did as leader of his country. _____

5) Whom did God help Uzziah to defeat? _____

6) What did Uzziah make in Jerusalem? _____

7) What did Uzziah do wrong? _____

8) What was the name of the priest who went after Uzziah? _____

9) Who were the only ones who were to burn incense before God? _____

10) For disobeying God, what did Uzziah receive? _____

11) What became lifted up when Uzziah was strong? _____

Inspirational Quote

"Unto the day of his death, some years later, Uzziah remained a leper—a living example of the folly of departing from a plain "Thus saith the Lord." Neither his exalted position nor his long life of service could be pleaded as an excuse for the presumptuous sin by which he marred the closing years of his reign, and brought upon himself the judgment of Heaven" (Ellen G. White, *Prophets and Kings* [Mountain View: Pacific Press Publishing Association, 1917], page 304)

A WICKED GRANDMOTHER

Hello, boys and girls. Does it seem like those who do wrong get away with it, which makes it seem okay for us to do as we please? But is it right to do as we please even if it is wrong? Would God be pleased with us if we behaved this way? Let's learn today about a mother named Athaliah. When she found out that her son Ahaziah had been killed, Athaliah, instead of doing what we would expect from a grieving mother, went on a killing spree. She killed every male who was in line for the throne (that is, anyone who had a claim to become the next king). But as God would have it, there was one boy, Joash, who escaped the killings. How? His aunt Jehosheba, who was married to the priest Jehoiada, hid Joash in a temple, away from his cruel grandmother Athaliah, for six years. After Athaliah had killed all the king's sons, she made herself ruler over the land of Judah.

Would a grandmother in this day and age do something so wicked just to become queen? Yes, little one. This world is very cold. There are many evil things that are done every day that we have no idea of. But we serve a God in heaven who knows everything. One day, everyone will receive their reward for what they have done during their lifetime.

So what happened to the prince Joash? When Joash was seven, Jehoiada the priest sent and fetched the captains over hundreds of soldiers and the guard. They were brought to him in the house of the Lord where he took an oath of them. Jehoiada then showed all these people Joash, the rightful heir to the throne, which Athaliah had captured. The priest then gave instructions as to what part each person should play. One third of the men were to guard the king's house. Another third was to guard the temple gate called Sur. And another third was to be at the gate behind the guard. They were also to surround the king, every man with their weapons in their hand. Anyone that came within range was to be killed and they were to be with the king at all times. Jehoida also gave the captains, weapons that had once belonged to king David that were now in the temple.

After everything was arranged, young Joash was anointed as king and a crown was placed on his head. With this, a great big noise went out from the people as they rejoiced in the crowning of seven-year-old Joash as their king. The noise was so loud that Queen Athaliah heard it. She came quickly to where the sound was coming from. When Athaliah looked in the temple, she saw the king and all the people with their musical instruments. What did Athaliah do now? She tore her clothes and cried out, "Treason! Treason!" Treason is the act of overthrowing a government. At this point, Jehoiada the priest brought out the captains and told them to follow Athaliah and kill her with the sword, but not inside the temple of the Lord. So the soldiers laid hands on Queen Athaliah and took her outside. When they got to the gate where the king's horses were kept, they killed her there.

Ah, little one, what a sad ending to a stolen seven years of prosperous living, doing as you please, ordering people around, and getting your own way with no one to tell you no. What do we learn from this, then— that we might do wicked things and flourish? When we live this way, it might seem like everything is going good for a while, but then calamity strikes. You see, little one, God is not sleeping. One day we will all have to face the judgment of God. As for Athaliah, she got away with murder for seven years, but in the end she was murdered. Little one, let's be happy with what God gives us. Don't steal others' property simply because you want it. Don't kill others so you can lay your hands on the fruits of another person's labor. Be content with what you have.

QUIZ #5

1) Who made herself queen over Judah? _____

2) What was the name of the baby who was saved from death? _____

3) Where was he hidden for six years? _____

4) Who was the aunt of Joash? _____

5) Who sent for the soldiers to come to the temple? _____

6) How old was Joash when he was crowned king? _____

7) To whom did the weapons given to the soldiers once belong? _____

8) What brought Athaliah to the temple? _____

9) What did she cry when she saw what was happening? _____

10) Did Athaliah continue to rule as queen? _____

11) What did the soldiers do to her? _____

12) Who is always watching what we are doing? _____

13) Should we do others harm so we can take their things? _____

Inspirational Quote

"Some years after coming to the throne, Jehoshaphat, now in the height of his prosperity, consented to the marriage of his son Jehoram to Athaliah, daughter of Ahab and Jezebel. By this union there was formed between the kingdoms of Judah and Israel an alliance which was not in the order of God, and which in times of crises brought disaster to the king of Judah and to many of his subjects" (Ellen G. White, "Jehoshaphat— No. 2," *Review and Herald* [December 25, 1913]).

A Little Too Far

Hello, boys and girls. Do you think your parents are too old-fashioned, that they need to loosen up and become modern? Do you believe that they should allow you to choose your friends, let you go to parties, allow you to dress in the latest fashion, and let you live as you choose? If they did this, then would they be perfect parents? Let's take a look at the Bible and find out about a girl who went just a little too far from her parents.

This girl was Dinah, daughter of Jacob and Leah. Dinah was not an only child, as she had eleven brothers. Today we would think it must have been hard to live in Dinah's house, where her mother lived with her father, his three other wives, and their children. And if this was not bad enough, one of the other wives was Dinah's mother's sister (Dinah's aunt). With Dinah having such a large family, one could believe that she might have felt lonely for female company her own age. Let's find out what happened to her.

Genesis 34:1 reads, "And Dinah the daughter of Leah, which she bare unto Jacob, went out to see the daughters of the land." Here we are told that Dinah had friends outside her family, who served the true God of heaven. She became friends with girls who did not serve God, as they were worldly. We don't know how Dinah acted when she was with her friends. The Bible says in Genesis 34:2 that Shechem, the prince of the country, saw Dinah and, upon looking at her, felt lustful. The Bible goes on to say that Shechem took hold of Dinah and raped her. When Shechem did this thing, he initially had no intention of marrying her, but after he had lain with her, his heart was moved with feelings of love for her and he spoke kindly to her. We might say this was a good thing. After all, Shechem was a prince. He was rich and could do much for Dinah in a worldly sense. But is that how her father would view this situation? Let's see.

Shechem goes to his father, Hamor, and tells him to get Dinah for his wife. In other words, he wanted permission from Dinah's father to marry her. Sounds very good, doesn't it? But Jacob did not see this as we today might see it. He was displeased that Shechem, a man who did not serve God, had raped his daughter, Dinah. So what did Jacob do? When his sons came back from the field, he told them what had happened. The brothers were sad, and then they became very angry because Shechem had done something that should never have been done. But Hamor begged on behalf of his son, saying that Shechem truly loved Dinah and wanted to do the right thing by marrying her. Then he went further, saying, "Your people should make marriages with our people. That way, you can live in this land with us, work here, and get things here."

Shechem now pleaded with Jacob to allow him to marry Dinah, who was already in his house. He promised that whatever was told him to do, he would do it. The sons of Jacob answered Shechem and Hamor dishonestly. They told them that it was not right for their sister to marry someone who was uncircumcised. But if every male of your country were to be circumcised, then we would give our daughters to you and take your daughters as our wives. We will live with you and we would become one people. But if you will not be circumcised, then we will take our daughter and will be gone.

These words were very pleasing to Shechem and his father and when they got back home, they told all the men of the city about being circumcised. The men listened to the words that were spoken to them and all of them were circumcised. As it happened, three days later, two of Jacob's sons, Simeon and Levi, took their swords, went into the city, killed all the men, and took their sister, Dinah, out of Shechem's house. They also took animals, children, women, and anything of value. Jacob was not pleased, because what his sons had done only made matters worse. So, little one, we see that all these problems came about because Dinah went out and made friends with worldly individuals. Had she not done so, she would not have been where Shechem could just snatch her up and do as he pleased with her. We can avoid danger by not courting it as Dinah did. Learn from her story, little one, learn!

QUIZ #6

1) Where in the Bible do we find this story? _____

2) Who were Dinah's parents? _____

3) How many brothers did Dinah have? _____

4) Who were Dinah's friends? _____

5) Who raped Dinah? _____

6) Who was Hamor? _____

7) After sleeping with Dinah, what did Shechem want to do? _____

8) What did Hamor say Jacob's people should do with his people? _____

9) What was Shechem to do in order to marry Dinah? _____

11) Which two sons of Jacob attacked the city and killed all the men? _____

Inspirational Quote

"He who seeks pleasure among those that fear not God is placing himself on Satan's ground and inviting his temptations" (Ellen G. White, *Patriarchs and Prophets* [Washington: Review and Herald Publishing Association, 1890], page 204)

THE LITTLE MAID

Greetings, little one. Have you ever done something for someone else but he or she never noticed it and didn't bother to thank you? If so, how did that make you feel? Did you think to yourself, *I'm never going to help that person again*? What would you do if you were the subject of the following story?

In the days of king Jehoram, Naaman, captain of the Syrian army, raided the land of Israel, captured a little girl, and took her to Syria. This little girl was given the job of serving Naaman's wife. Imagine, little one, if strangers, much less an army, came to your country, surrounded your town or village, came into your house, maybe killed some of your family members, and then captured you to take you away to be a servant forever in a foreign land. How would you feel? Would you want to do the best job you could for Mrs. Naaman? Would you want to tell these people anything at all about the God you served?

Well, as the story goes in 2 Kings 5, captain Naaman, as great and mighty as he was in battle, ended up with leprosy. This is a terrible disease that causes sores to appear on the skin. Leprosy can destroy the nerve endings in the hands and feet, causing loss of feeling, which makes the fingers and the toes start to peel away from the body until they just fall off, leaving the person deformed. Leprosy can also affect the nose, throat, and eyes, and can lead to paralysis and gangrene. Plus, it spreads easily to other people.

Wow, no wonder Naaman was very nervous about his problem. He was rich and had the best doctors that money could buy, but there was no cure for leprosy to be found anywhere in the world. Naaman felt hopeless. Even Mrs. Naaman knew that soon her husband must leave her forever. One day, Mrs. Naaman had a conversation with her little maid. Maybe she talked about the latest news from the doctors, mentioning how they had told Naaman how much longer he could live among people before he had to leave his home, family, and job behind and go live with the other lepers until he died.

On hearing this, the little maid, without hesitating, told her mistress, "Would it that God, my Lord, were not with the prophet who is in Samaria, for he would heal captain Naaman of his leprosy." Now Mrs. Naaman, upon hearing this, felt hope spring up in her heart. She ran off to tell her husband what the little maid had said. News came to the king of Syria, who gave Naaman permission to go seek help in the land of Israel. The story ended with Naaman's being healed of leprosy. Nowhere else in the Bible had anyone been healed of this disease, until the time of Jesus. Little one, Naaman was not even a Christian, yet because of what God ultimately did for him, beginning with the little maid, he gave his heart to God.

Now, what if that little maid had said to herself, *Humph! It serves captain Naaman right to have leprosy. That is God paying him back for troubling Israel, for capturing me, and for making me into a slave. Yes, die, die, you dog!* No, friend, this little maid was true to the God she served. When she heard about her master's illness, she felt sorry for him. And remembering the miracles that the prophet Elisha had done, she knew that Elisha could heal Naaman through the power of the God of heaven. Because of what the little maid did, a life was saved for God. We don't know what happened to the little maid after that, but we do know that she did what was right for Jesus. Will you be helpful for Jesus too, little one, and do your best, no matter how people hurt you? Matthew 5:12 reads, "Rejoice, and be exceeding glad: for great is your reward in heaven."

Quiz #7

1) Who was the prophet in Samaria? _____

2) Where in the Bible can this story be found? _____

3) What disease did Naaman have? _____

4) Describe two ways in which leprosy affects the body. _____

5) Who told Naaman's wife about where to get help? _____

6) Had anyone ever been healed of this sickness before? _____

7) When was the next time in the Bible that anyone was healed of leprosy? _____

8) What position did Naaman have? _____

9) Who sent Naaman away to get help? _____

10) Would Naaman had received healing if the little maid had not said something about Elisha? _____

11) Should we stop helping people because of how we feel? _____

12) Where is our reward to be found for our faithful service to Jesus? _____

Inspirational Quote

"We know not in what line our children may be called to serve. They may spend their lives within the circle of the home; they may engage in life's common vocations, or go as teachers of the gospel to heathen lands; but all are alike called to be missionaries for God, ministers of mercy to the world" (Ellen G. White, *Conflict and Courage* [Washington: Review and Herald Publishing Association, 1970], page 227)

A Jealous Sister

Boys and girls, do you feel that life is unfair to you, that you deserve better, and that no one can take your place? If someone comes along who is better at something than you are, do you feel hate in your heart toward that person? Well, let's take a look at a story to see how God looks at jealousy and gossiping.

A long time ago, God raised up a man by the name of Moses to lead the children of Israel from slavery in Egypt to a land that was flowing with milk and honey. When Moses was forty years old, before he was ready for the job of deliverer, he rose up and killed an Egyptian. After doing this, he had to run away from Egypt to save his life. While away, he met Jethro, the priest of Midian, and married one of his seven daughters, Zipporah. They had two sons.

When Moses was eighty years old, God called him to go back to Egypt and tell Pharaoh to let God's people go. Moses did not feel like he could do this, so God told him that his brother Aaron would be there as his mouthpiece to help speak to the pharaoh. Then God sent ten plagues and set the children of Israel free. While the Israelites were on their way to the Promised Land, Jethro took Zipporah and her two sons to join up with Moses once more.

Now you would think this would be a happy time. But while meeting with Moses, Jethro gave him some advice on how to organize the camp so that Moses would not become worn down by doing the work of judging over two million people. Chosen leaders were placed in charge of judging the people. How did Aaron and their sister, Miriam, feel about this change in the leadership of the camp?

In Numbers 12, we are told that Miriam was not too pleased with Moses's wife. Miriam called her an Ethiopian woman when she was a Midianite. So Miriam met with Aaron and voiced her feelings. She began to murmur and complain about Moses and his wife and about the new changes taking place in the camp. Now, little one, when someone comes to us with a story about another person and we do not know what that other person has to say about the matter, we should not take either party's side. It is wrong to share feelings of sympathy with one person when you do not know the whole story. So it was with Aaron. He listened to and sided with his sister, Miriam, rather than letting her know it was wrong of her to have such feelings.

While all of this was going on, God was listening. And suddenly the Lord said to Moses that he should gather Aaron and Miriam and that all three of them should come and meet God at the tabernacle. When all three came, the Lord called for Aaron and Miriam and said that normally he would make himself known to a prophet by way of visions and dreams, but such was not the case with Moses. "To him I speak face-to-face. Now, Aaron and Miriam, why were you not afraid to speak against my servant, Moses?"

When God said these words, Aaron and Miriam were both speechless. The Bible says that the anger of the Lord was against them. When the Lord departed from among them, Miriam was leprous and as white as snow. When Aaron looked at his sister, he saw that she had leprosy, so he begged Moses to forgive them for their sin of speaking foolishly against him and to ask God for Miriam to be healed. Once Moses did as he was asked, the Lord told him to put Miriam outside the camp for seven days and that after that she could be let back in. So, little one, we see that God does not approve of our having evil feelings in our hearts and then taking our feelings out on other people. May God help us to overcome murmuring!

Quiz #8

1) Who was Moses's sister? _____

2) Which country did God deliver the children of Israel from? _____

3) How old was Moses when he killed an Egyptian? _____

4) Who was Moses's wife? _____

5) What was the occupation of Jethro? _____

6) Who met Moses on the way to the Promised Land? _____

7) What nationality was Zipporah? _____

8) Who sympathized with Miriam? _____

9) Whom did God speak face-to-face with? _____

10) What did Miriam receive for her murmuring and complaining? _____

11) How long was Miriam put out of the camp? _____

Inspirational Quote

"The judgment visited upon Miriam should be a rebuke to all who yield to jealousy, and murmur against those upon whom God lays the burden of His work" (Ellen G. White, *Conflict and Courage* [Washington: Review and Herald Publishing Association, 1970], page 104)

One Man's Obedience

Little one, do you want Jesus in your life? Here is a good reason why you should want him in your life. Genesis 6:5–6 reads, "And God saw that the wickedness of man was great in the earth, and that every imagination of the thoughts of his heart was only evil continually. And it repented the Lord that he had made man on the earth, and it grieved him at his heart." Here was a time when the people who lived on earth became so wicked that God felt sorry that he had made humankind. Little one, is Jesus pleased with the things that you do?

What was God going to do about this problem? Genesis 6:7 reads, "And the Lord said, I will destroy man whom I have created from the face of the earth; both man, and beast, and the creeping thing, and the fowls of the air; for it repenteth me that I have made them." But as God looked throughout the earth, he saw that there was one man who was not wicked, who loved the Lord, and who was happy to serve him. This man was Noah.

Genesis 6:13–14 reads, "And God said unto Noah, The end of all flesh is come before me; for the earth is filled with violence through them; and, behold, I will destroy them with the earth. Make thee an ark of gopher wood; rooms shalt thou make in the ark, and shalt pitch it within and without with pitch." God did not give Noah any money to build this ark, yet Noah never complained about the work given him. Instead, he went right to work with his family in building this big boat. During this time, a span of 120 years, Noah preached to the people, saying, "Get ready! You must get on board, for God is going to destroy this earth with a flood of waters, and only those on board will be saved." But many of the people laughed and made fun of Noah, saying that he was crazy. You see, little one, water had never fallen from the sky before, and the people thought that God loved them too much to destroy them and the world.

Well, one day the ark was finished. God said to Noah, "Come thou and all thy house into the ark; for thee have I seen righteous before me in this generation. Of every clean beast thou shalt take to thee by sevens, the male and his female: and of beasts that are not clean by two, the male and his female" (Genesis 7:1–2). Can you imagine what the people must have thought when they saw this amazing sight? Wild animals, terrible beasts, were getting into the ark two by two. Birds of all sizes were flying straight into the ark. The insects went marching on too. And yet the heart of man was too stubborn to obey God.

How many days were Noah's family and the animals on board the ark before the rains began? Genesis 7:4 reads, "For yet seven days, and I [God] will cause it to rain upon the earth forty days and forty nights; and every living substance that I have made will I destroy from off the face of the earth." During these seven days, the people did not stop their wicked ways. They continued to make Noah the main point of their jokes. What happened after the seven days? As it says in Genesis 7:10, "And it came to pass after seven days, that the waters of the flood were upon the earth." It had rained for forty days and forty nights. How had Noah, his family, and all the animals stayed safe while they were riding in a boiling sea filled with rocks, trees, etc.? As is stated in Genesis 7:16, "The Lord shut him in," meaning that God kept them all safe inside the ark. Little one, by having faith in God, Noah and his family were kept safe in the ark. Do you know that God will shut you in today too, if you just let him? His arms are just as willing to save you now as they were when he saved Noah and his family.

QUIZ #9

1) Who was the only man on the earth that God found who was not wicked? _____

2) What did God see that grieved his heart? _____

3) What did God decide to do with humankind and the beasts? _____

4) What did God tell Noah to build? _____

5) How long did it rain during the flood? _____

6) Who told Noah when it was time to get on the ark? _____

7) Besides Noah, name something that went on board. _____

8) How long after everything was on board did the rain begin? _____

9) What type of wood was used to build the ark? _____

10) What kept Noah and his family safe while every other human being died? _____

Inspirational Quote

"'And the Lord shut him in.' The massive door, which it was impossible for those within to close, was slowly swung to its place by unseen hands. Noah was shut in, and the rejecters of God's mercy were shut out. The seal of Heaven was on that door; God had shut it, and God alone could open it" (Ellen G. White, *Conflict and Courage* [Washington: Review and Herald Publishing Association, 1970], page 39)

GOING FIRST

Hello, little one. Do you know anyone who is unkind to others, who only thinks of him- or herself and what he or she wants? Hey, maybe that describes you. Let's see what we can learn from good old Abraham (who is referred to in the following Bible quotations as Abram). Genesis 12:1 reads, "Now the Lord had said unto Abram, Get thee out of thy country, and from thy kindred, and from thy father's house, unto a land that I will shew thee." So, little one, God told Abram to get out of his country and leave his family's house in order to go to a land that he did not know.

Abram obeyed the Lord and moved. Genesis 13:5 reads, "And Abram took Sarai his wife, and Lot his brother's son, and all their substance that they had gathered, and the souls that they had gotten in Haran; and they went forth to go into the land of Canaan; and into the land of Canaan they came." So along with Abram's wife went Lot, his nephew. What does the Bible say about the lifestyle of Abram? Genesis 13:2 reads, "And Abram was very rich in cattle, in silver, and in gold." What about Lot? Genesis 13:5 reads, "And Lot also, which went with Abram, had flocks, and herds, and tents." How did they all get along? As it says in Genesis 13:7, "And there was a strife between the herdmen of Abram's cattle and the herdmen of Lot's cattle." Why was there a quarrel? Genesis 13:6 has the answer: "And the land was not able to bear them, that they might dwell together: for their substance was great, so that they could not dwell together." Abram and Lot both had so many animals that their servants were fighting over the land needed to feed those animals.

Wow, this is a big problem. What should they do? Genesis 13:8–9 says this: "And Abram said unto Lot, Let there be no strife, I pray thee, between me and thee. … Is not the whole land before thee? Separate thyself, I pray thee, from me: if thou wilt take the left hand, then I will go to the right; or if thou depart to the right hand, then I will go to the left." Does that sound right to you, little one? We know that Abram was the oldest, so with Lot being the younger and the one to whom God had not given the land, what do you think he should do?

Genesis 13:10–12 reads, "And Lot lifted up his eyes, and beheld all the plain of Jordan, that it was well watered everywhere, … Then Lot chose him all the plain of Jordan; … Abram dwelled in the land of Canaan, and Lot dwelled in the cities of the plain, and pitched his tent toward Sodom." Remember what we talked about at the beginning of this chapter? Here we see that Lot did not say, "No, Uncle Abram. God promised this land to you. You choose first, and I will go the other way." Oh no, Lot took the offer, looked around, and chose the best piece of land—land that was green and well watered for his flocks—and left the dry, thirsty desert to his uncle.

Do you do selfish things, little one? Do you do only what seems right to you? Do you care about others' feelings? Does Jesus want you to be mean and unkind to others? If you are, then pray and ask Jesus to help you to be kind and loving, just like Abraham.

Now, little one, even though Lot chose the best part of the land for his flocks, look at what he did not know. Genesis 13:14 tell us, "But the men of Sodom were wicked and sinners before the Lord exceedingly." Lot did not know that even though the land was good, the people living there were evil. We cannot go by how good a thing looks on the outside. Instead, we need Jesus to guide us always in making the right decision. Let's learn to pray before we act. Jesus will help us.

QUIZ #10

1) Besides his wife, which family member went with Abram when he left his home? _____

2) Who told Abram to move? _____

3) What was Abram rich in? _____

4) What did Lot have? _____

5) Why were the servants of Abram and Lot quarreling? _____

6) Who suggested that they should separate? _____

7) Who placed his tent toward Sodom? _____

8) When Lot separated from Abram, where did Abram dwell? _____

9) How does the Bible describe the men of Sodom? _____

10) Did Lot make a good choice? _____

11) To whom did God promise the land of Canaan? _____

12) Should we be mean and behave selfishly toward others? _____

Inspirational Quote

"There are many ways which lead to Sodom. We all need anointed eyesight, that we may discern the way that leads to God" (Ellen G. White, *Christ Triumphant* [Hagerstown: Review and Herald Publishing Association, 1999), page 72)

What's in a Name?

Greetings, little one. How many names do you have? Do names have meanings? Did you know that a lot of the people in the Bible had only one name? Can you think of anyone in the Bible who had one name? Genesis 4:25 reads, "And Adam knew his wife again; and she bare a son, and called his name Seth: For God, said she, hath appointed me another seed instead of Abel, whom Cain slew." Here Adam and Eve called their third son Seth, which means "appointed." Seth was given by God in place of his brother Abel, whom Cain killed.

Now how about the name Jesus? What does that mean? Matthew 1:21 reads, "And she shall bring forth a son, and thou shalt call his name Jesus: for he shall save his people from their sins." Jesus was to save the people from their sins, or he was to be their Savior. So the name Jesus means "Savior." What about his other name, Christ? John 1:41 reads, "He first findeth his own brother Simon, and saith unto him, We have found the Messias, which is, being interpreted, the Christ." *Christ* means "Messiah," which means "Anointed." So Jesus Christ is the Anointed One, the Savior. When people call him Christ Jesus, they are saying "the Anointed Savior." Even to say "Jesus the Christ" is to say "Savior, the Anointed One." So whenever we use the name of Jesus, it points us to what he is doing for us: He is our Savior, the only one who can save us from our sins. This is why it is foolish to serve any idols, things that we love more than God, as none of these things can save us from death.

But, little one, are these the only names of Jesus in the Bible? Let's see. John 15:5 reads, "I [Jesus] am the vine, ye are the branches." Jesus is also called the Vine, and those who accept him as their Lord and Savior are his branches. Are you a part of Jesus's family, little one? John 1:29 reads, "The next day John seeth Jesus coming unto him, and saith, Behold the Lamb of God, which taketh away the sin of the world." Jesus is also called the Lamb of God. Why? As an innocent lamb, he died for the guilty, the entire human family.

In Revelation 19:16 we read, "And he hath on his vesture and on his thigh a name written, King of Kings, and Lord of Lords." Jesus is also King of every king, and Lord over all lords. As King, he is worthy of our service. Would you like to be one of his followers, little one?

How about in the Old Testament—do we find any names for Jesus there? Song of Solomon 2:1 reads, "I am the rose of Sharon, and the lily of the valleys." Oh yes, Jesus is the rose of Sharon and the lily of the valley.

Little one, the point is that we need Jesus, the Rose of Sharon, in our lives to help us have a beautiful character. He will help to keep us pure while we are living in this world of sin.

Little one, let us pray and ask Jesus to help us to have a good name as well, the name of "Christian." Thank you, Jesus!

QUIZ #11

1) Whose name means "appointed"? _____

2) What does the name Jesus Christ mean? _____

3) What is Jesus called in Revelation 19:16? _____

4) In which book of the Bible is Jesus called the rose of Sharon? _____

5) Besides the name Christ, what is another name for "Anointed"? _____

6) What does John call Jesus? _____

7) If Jesus is the Vine, then what are his followers? _____

8) Who is to save people from their sins? _____

9) In which book of the Bible are we told to call him Jesus? _____

10) What good name should we desire to have today? _____

Inspirational Quote

"No sooner is the name of Jesus mentioned in love and tenderness than angels of God draw near, to soften and subdue the heart" (Ellen G. White, *Colporteur Ministry* [Mountain View: Pacific Press Publishing Association, 1953], page 111)

THE BOASTFUL KING

Do you often go around telling people what you have or what your parents have? There was a king in the Bible whose name was Hezekiah. He was a good king, one who did what was right in the sight of the Lord. "What did he do?" you ask. Based on 2 Chronicles 29–30, he repaired the temple of God, put back the vessels, and brought back the priests of the Lord to serve. Those priests held the Passover service. Yes, little one, King Hezekiah led the people to seek the Lord.

Now what could possibly go wrong for someone like this? The Bible goes on to say that Hezekiah became sick with a terrible disease for which there was no cure. He was going to die. God sent the prophet Isaiah to him with the message that he should prepare himself, for he would die. How would you feel, little one, if God told you that you were going to die? I would say that you'd feel very sad and hopeless. Because King Hezekiah felt sad and hopeless after hearing this, he turned his face to the wall and prayed to God, begging God to remember the good things that he had done. And then he broke down, crying bitterly. Well, his tears moved the heart of God. Before Isaiah had left the palace, God told him to go back and tell the king, "I have heard your prayer, I have seen your tears, I will heal you and I will add fifteen years to your life." Hallelujah. Glory to God for his goodness to the king.

The prophet Isaiah goes on to tell the king to take a lump of figs, make a plaster, lay it on his boil and he would recover. Once Hezekiah did this, he was healed. But, little one, Hezekiah went on to ask about what sign God would show him to let him know that he would be healed. Isaiah asked him to choose: "Do you want the shadow of the sun to go forward ten degrees or go back ten degrees?" The king chose for it to go back. Unknown to them both, in the land of Babylon were scientists who had an instrument that kept up with the movement of the sun: a sundial. So when the sign for Hezekiah appeared, namely, the sun's going back ten degrees, it was shown on this sundial, which caused the Babylonians, who were far away, to wonder what had happened.

The Babylonians knew of no person who had the power to make the sun move backward; only the God of heaven could do so. And since only the Israelites worshipped the God of heaven, the Babylonians determined that those people would be the only ones who would know what had happened. Berodach-baladan, king of

Babylon, sent men to Hezekiah with a present, in the hopes of having their question answered. But when the men came to the king, Hezekiah turned into a show-off. He showed the men all the precious things in his house, the gold, silver, spices, and ointments—plus the house where he kept his armor and all his treasures. Little one, he showed them everything that he had.

When the men left, the prophet Isaiah visited the king and asked him, "What did these men see in your house?" When the king told Isaiah that they had seen everything in his house, including all his treasures, Isaiah delivered the Lord's message to the king that the day would come when all that was in his house would be carried away into Babylon. Nothing would be left. Hezekiah made a big mistake, little one: he had said nothing about God's goodness in healing him from his terrible disease, and nothing about how God had turned the sun back, which would have led the Babylonians to worship the true and living God. How sad, little one, that King Hezekiah did not honor God in front of people of the world but only thought about himself.

Little one, do you want to boast? If so, then follow King David's advice in Psalm 44:8: "In God we boast all the day long, and praise thy name for ever."

Quiz #12

1) Which prophet was sent with a message to Hezekiah? _____

2) Name one thing that Hezekiah did that pleased the Lord. _____

3) What did God see that moved his heart? _____

4) What was Hezekiah to put on his boil? _____

5) Who was the king of Babylon at this time? _____

6) Who asked for a sign? _____

7) What was the sign? _____

8) What instrument was used to tell time by a shadow? _____

9) What nation was using this instrument? _____

10) Name two things that the king showed the visitors. _____

11) Was Hezekiah sharing the gospel or showing off his goods? _____

12) Did Hezekiah give the credit to God for the sign of the sun? _____

13) Is God pleased when we show off for other people? _____

Inspirational Quote

"The visit of these messengers from the ruler of a far-away land gave Hezekiah an opportunity to extol the living God. How easy it would have been for him to tell them of God, the upholder of all created things, through whose favor his own life had been spared when all other hope had fled! What momentous transformations might have taken place had these seekers after truth from the plains of Chaldea been led to acknowledge the supreme sovereignty of the living God. But pride and vanity took possession of Hezekiah's heart, and in self-exaltation he laid open to covetous eyes the treasures with which God had enriched his people. ...Not to glorify God did he do this, but to exalt himself in the eyes of the foreign princes" (Ellen G. White, *Prophets and Kings* [Mountain View: Pacific Press Publishing Association, 1917], page 344)

QUIZ ANSWERS

QUIZ # 1: (The Lie that went Wrong)

1) 1 Kings 14 2) Jeroboam 3) her clothes 4) see 5) the Lord 6) no 7) Abijah
8) David 9) worship false gods 10) the moment his mother's feet entered the city
11) Satan 12) heaven 13) no

QUIZ # 2: (A Bad Choice)

1) Mark 10:17-22 2) the rich young ruler 3) what shall I do to inherit eternal life?
4) the commandments 5) one 6) sell what he had and give to the poor 7) to keep his riches 8) sorrowful 9) no 10) the love of God in his heart

QUIZ # 3: (A Special Book)

1) more than 40 writers 2) the printing press 3) 1600 years 4) the bible 5) no
6) every Bible burned 7) Christianity 8) French philosopher Voltaire 9) the Geneva Bible Society 10) no 11) Johannes Gutenberg

QUIZ # 4: (Full of Pride)

1) 2 Chronicles 26 2) 16 3) he obeyed God 4) built towers in Jerusalem and dug many wells 5) the Philistines and the Arabians 6) engines 7) went into the temple to burn incense 8) Azariah 9) the priests 10) leprosy 11) his heart

QUIZ # 5: (A Wicked Grandmother)

1) Athaliah 2) Joash 3) in the temple 4) Jehosheba 5) Jehoiada 6) seven 7) king David 8) a great big noise from the people 9) treason 10) no 11) kill her with the sword 12) God 13) no

QUIZ # 6: (A Little Too Far)

1) Genesis 34 2) Jacob and Leah 3) eleven 4) the daughters of the land 5) Shechem
6) Shechem's father 7) marry her 8) make marriages 9) he had to be circumcised
10) Simeon and Levi

QUIZ # 7: (The Little Maid)

1) Elisha 2) 2 Kings 5 3) leprosy 4) sores on the skin, nerve endings in the hands and feet are destroyed 5) the little maid 6) no 7) the time of Christ 8) captain of the Syrian army 9) the king of Syria 10) no, but God has many ways 11) no 12) in heaven

QUIZ # 8: (A Jealous Sister)

1) Miriam 2) Egypt 3) 40 years 4) Zipporah 5) priest of Midian 6) Jethro, Zipporah and Moses' two sons 7) Midianite 8) Aaron 9) Moses 10) leprosy 11) seven days

QUIZ # 9: (One Man's Obedience)

1) Noah 2) the wickedness of man that it was great in the earth 3) destroy them 4) an ark 5) 40 days and 40 nights 6) God 7) clean beasts 8) seven days 9) gopher wood 10) faith in God

QUIZ # 10: (Going First)

1) Lot, his nephew 2) the Lord 3) cattle, silver and gold 4) flocks, herds and tents 5) the land was not able to bear them so they could dwell together 6) Abram 7) Lot 8) in the land of Canaan 9) wicked and sinners before the Lord exceedingly 10) no 11) Abram 12) no

QUIZ # 11: (What's in a Name?)

1) Seth 2) Savior Anointed 3) King of Kings and Lord of Lords 4) Song of Solomon 5) Messiah 6) Lamb of God 7) the branches 8) Jesus 9) Matthew 10) Christian

QUIZ # 12: (The Boastful King)

1) Isaiah 2) repaired the temple of God 3) the tears of Hezekiah 4) a lump of figs 5) Berodach-baladan 6) king Hezekiah 7) the shadow of the sun to go back 10 degrees 8) a sun dial 9) Babylon 10) gold and silver 11) showing off his goods 12) no 13) no

About the Author

Donna Hackett has no children of her own but has been blessed by God to work with children of all ages in a few places around the world. She did not set out to do this kind of work, but one day, after seeing a need to help adults who could not read, she and her husband started a learn-to-read program in their home. On the night that classes were to begin, not one adult showed up—but about fifty children from the surrounding neighborhood did. From this began a little evening school by which the Lord taught Donna how to relate to children: how to interact with them, listen to them, and even ask them questions about how they would deal with different real-life situations. After Donna had done this, the Lord assigned her to work with one hundred children from three to five years old in a school. She was to have morning devotion with them and teach them about God, as they each came from a turbulent environment. This she did by the help of God, and from this the children learned how to pray. They also learned about God from the stories of the Bible. When this program came to an end, the Lord opened another door for Donna, to help a church school not far from her home, where she would have devotion and share the Bible with the children there. This went so well that the head teacher arranged for her to do a children's week-of-prayer program at the church for the entire community. The Lord blessed this endeavor. Each night, more and more children and youth would come. Today, Donna is still sharing these Bible stories with children at her local church, twice every month. It is Donna's prayer and hope that this same love for spiritual things will be cultivated in all those who should read these few stories in this little volume.

ABOUT THE BOOK

This is a book filled with teachings about morals and the principles of God. It is for old and young alike. The wonderful thing about the word of God is that it has no age limit; instead, it is for everyone. Many adults have read *Little Lambs Bible Story Time* and have come back to the author to voice their opinion of how they loved reading the stories themselves, as they now looked at them in a different light, through the eyes of a child. When you stop and think about the many lessons that these stories can teach, you can see that your children should be brought up with better guidance. Parents must take the time to teach their children the ways of righteousness. These stories are designed, by the grace of God, to help parents present lessons to their children and hopefully start conversations with them to help in their growth process and show them how to make the right decisions.

AuthorHouse™
1663 Liberty Drive
Bloomington, IN 47403
www.authorhouse.com
Phone: 1 (800) 839-8640

Scripture quotations are from the Holy Bible, King James Version (Authorized Version). First published in 1611. Quoted from the KJV Classic Reference Bible, Copyright © 1983 by the Zondervan Corporation.

Published by AuthorHouse: 06/13/2016

ISBN: 978-1-5246-0972-6 (sc)
978-1-5246-0973-3 (e)

Library of Congress Control Number: 2016908239

Print information available on the last page.

Any people depicted in stock imagery provided by Thinkstock are models, and such images are being used for illustrative purposes only. Certain stock imagery © Thinkstock.

This book is printed on acid-free paper.

authorHOUSE®

Printed in the United States
By Bookmasters